Inner-course

Inner-course

A Plea for Real Love

Toni Blackman

Villard | New York

All rights reserved under International and Pan-American Copyright Conven-
tions. Published in the United States by Villard Books, an imprint of
The Random House Publishing Group, a division of Random House, Inc.,
New York, and simultaneously in Canada by Random House of Canada Lim-
ited, Toronto.

VILLARD BOOKS and "V" CIRCLED Design are registered trademarks of
Random House, Inc.

Library of Congress Cataloging-in-Publication Data

Blackman, Toni.
    Inner-course : a plea for real love / by Toni Blackman.
        p. cm.
ISBN 0-375-50914-3
1. African American women—Poetry. 2. Love poetry, American. I. Title.
PS3602.L3253I56 2003
811'.6—dc21
2003047992

Villard Books website address: www.villard.com

Printed in the United States of America on acid-free paper

9 8 7 6 5 4 3 2

FIRST EDITION

Book design by Ralph L. Fowler

Dedicated to E. Ethelbert Miller,

whose devotion to poetry and poets has made our

world a better place to be. There are no words to express

the magnitude of my gratitude. There is no way I

could ever repay you for the impact you have

made on my life so I simply write the words:

thank you.

And to Gil Scott-Heron,

the first poet with whose voice I fell in love—

before I could even walk.

THANK-YOUS

I shall attempt to avoid sounding like the roll-call
shout-out on the radio, but big up to Aunt Jen-
nifer for what she started when I was a just a little
girl. Thanks, Mom, for growing *with* me. All of
my aunts, uncles, cousins . . . Professor Vera Katz,
Deborah Menkart, Dr. Sherrill Johnson, Kim
Chan, Baraka, Linda, Maureen, Liz Lerman,
Jennifer Nelson, Balu Littleton, Kathy Freshley,
Melissa Bradley; the Fresh Girls—Terri and
Mayor Yvonne Beals; Kevin Powell, Baye, Geoff,
Alejandro, Ras, Jelani Cobb, Omar Tyree,
Carlisle, April, Adrea, Troy White, Chris W.,
Dawna Ballard; I.E.: Joni Jones, Cornelius, Flor-
ence, Tuesday, Charles, Brian, John, Kanili,
Depelsha; Neta, Sandy, Michele B., Reverend
Yolanda, Tumara, Jinah, Deidra, Val, Kim; Janice
and Tracy; Toye, Michelle Spence, Tamara and
Mrs. Francois, Sydney; S.A.: Dzino and Rage,
Shaheen, Kgafela, Widada, James P., Windybrow,
Blaize; France: Shay, Quew, Lord Jazz,
Raymond, Tania, Nadine, Guilluame, Nino,
Fabrice, Pascal, Aline; U.K.: Mannafest, Geral-
dine, Jonzi, Ty, Malaika, Charlie, Temi; SEN:
Adama, Baba, Cire, Bebe, Serigne, Jean Paul and
Karen, Gallo, Patrick, Dame; Kwame, Kenny C.,
Brian G., Silvana, Psalm, Munch, Tone, Cheles,

Bobby Hill, Imani; Dr. Mbaye Cham, Nikongo, Cummings, Stroman, Wright, Woods, Roberta McLeod, Sybil; Jeff Goins; Vivian Chew; Nkiru; Abiodun; Debbie Cowell; Susan Taylor.

NABFEME, HU Fam, 9:30 Club, Dodge Foundation, Echoing Green Foundation, WPAS, WHUR 96.3 Spoken Word Cafe, Lois and the Nuyorican Poets Cafe, the Freestyle Union, Zulu Nation, Filli Foundation, Dr. Deben, Dumisani, Queen Afua, Harvey Herman, Landmark Education, Iyanla Vanzant, InnerVisions, Ethelbert, Kalamu ya Salaam, Miguel Algarín, Eugene Redmond, Carolyn Rodgers, Bob Holman, Laini Mataka, Sonia Sanchez, Sharon Olds, Billy Collins, Amiri Baraka, Sekou, Maya, Nikki, Beau Sia, Willie Perdomo, Suheir, Jessica, Rha, Roger, Craig Harris, Jay Rodriguez, Ezra, Terence Nicholson, Cousin Carla and Cousin Lisa; Aunt Bennye, we did it. Daddy, seeing you helps me see myself. I love you.

And for being yourself: Meshell, Bahamadia, Camille, Erykah, Jill, India, Jean Grae, Lauryn, N'Dambi, Navasha, Alexis, Tamar Kali, Imani Uzuri—you inspire me.

And for your patience: my editor, Melody Guy; my agent, Susan Raihofer; and the entire staff at Villard.

CONTENTS

i love short takes . . .

i love taggin' your heart . . .

INNER-COURSE (INTRODUCTION)

How does one reflect on the need for love out there in the world without reflecting on the inner-love that might be lacking? How does one insist that others be just and fair without being just and fair oneself? At the onset of this project I began an internal cleansing of negative thoughts and feelings about others and myself. In the midst of pulling together poems and introspective writings, the paper became a mirror. At times the sight of myself was inspiring and at others ugly from the inside out, but at all times it's been affirming, life-affirming. I am alive, breathing, learning and growing.

When one delves beyond producing work for mere entertainment, beyond generating material for intellectual satisfaction, one is choosing the path to higher self. This journey requires much more sweat than the others, the tears are more frequent, and the ever-present aroma of the truth can burn the nostrils. It's an incredible space to be in and one of my greatest challenges. I can see why it might take a lifetime to complete even a small book.

My Inner-course involves learning to be silent and how to be comfortable in that space. It has been humbling to say the least. The silence has allowed me to hear my tone of voice, which is sometimes not loving; to hear the gossip that slips too easily from my lips; and to hear the voices of self-doubt still lingering right beneath the surface of my seemingly confident skin. Yet in this same space of self-reflection I learn the art of self-forgiveness and the power of confession and how much stronger I am for admitting, acknowledging my weaknesses. The perfectionist embracing the idea of being human has been constant.

The cynical side of my spirit is attempting to let go of one of my favorite quotes: "I love humanity, it's the people I can't stand." The less mature, less evolved me is attempting to accept the people that cross my path for who, what, and, most important, *where* they are. Kenny Carroll, a big brother poet of mine, used to say that poets are the conscience of the people. Consciousness requires courage, because to be authentic is to be free from cowardice. To be a poet is to take a stand.

The work in this collection was created over the last ten years or so and represents different phases of my development as not only a writer, but as a woman and a human being. It is an interesting space to be in, to open a book and discover yourself, to read small pieces of your history and the world around you. *Inner-course* is essentially a collection of love poems and writings about love because that is what I wish to release into the universe. The most important decision we will make in our lives is to love or not.

I remember taking my first poems to my mentor, E. Ethelbert Miller, and his first challenge to me as a writer. He talked about the need for self-exposure, the need for the nakedness of words and how to write the piece even though Shawn or Aunt Bell will know you are writing about them. I remember the conversations about our culture and our connections to the past. I remember the conversations about what it means to be an artist. Those conversations, a critical part of my Inner-course, changed my life.

I hope that somewhere on some page, or maybe between one of the lines, each person who reads through this might find a piece of himself or herself, a smile, a tear, or something to share with someone else. Inner-course is something we all have. Thank you for sharing this part of the journey with me.

i hate valentine's day

it's nothing personal against
cupid or the little curly haired
girl on cards and decorations

i definitely don't have anything
against chocolate candy, roses
or the color red

it's just that like so many
other holidays it feeds on the
loneliness of the always consuming
consumer

valentine's day is big business
in america

and ain't nothing to do with love

two too many fall prey to the hype
getting trapped in crowded rooms
full of nothing no one, but
a temporary fix for what's
really ailing them

this let me give you some loving
once a year thing just does not fly

i prefer people who make me smile every day

and who is this mr. valentine's

and why is cupid naked
and who wants to be shot with a damn
bow and arrow

does anyone know or
does it even matter

i mean, we're all suckers anyway
celebrating holidays and days that
don't move us forward

riding emotional ferris wheels
going round and round
and we pay people to sit there

this poem is a cry a plea
love is not to be bought or sold
it's like air and water
a necessity

stuck in the air
sun and wind in our eyes
we cannot see

because we're looking
for love

in all the wrong places
in all the wrong spaces
instead of in our own faces

i love tellin' stories . . .

freedom piece

Immersed in a pool of chaos and confusion, fearful of freedom, scared of peace and afraid of living in a so-called civilized world, I reach out for something other than what is being offered to me. My efforts are labeled radical, categorized as abnormal, and seen as a waste of time. Dreams are for the night, they tell me. They want me to embrace the sky as only a home for clouds, but I want to reside there, at least temporarily, dancing winged and free among the birds singing for one another. The music of the skies belongs to each of us, to newborn babies, to the elderly and everyone in between. What kind of existence pays homage to those that came before us, to those that sacrificed so that we might breathe freely? Is it one of complacency, do nothingness and waiting for change? Or is it that which suggests that I might be the very thing the world waits for, that I might possess the recipe or hold the key?

hold me

my fears rise like
bath water in our small tub
the closer your breath is
to the nape of my neck
the hotter i feel
as the perspiration rides
the tip of my nose
your well-intentioned embrace
causes watery eyes and
heart races beating in
time to the sound of my cries
your hands big and warm
cupped together serve as the
perfect reservoir reminding me
of what i've been thirsty for
carefully cautiously
i slowly sip your warmth

well . . .

the longing feels like loss
although we remain connected
i cannot see you or touch your face

wondering where we will meet
with all the bombs exploding
with all the planes crashing
into buildings
it feels as if this lovin'
has become high risk

commitment phobia
seems irrelevant
career dreams secondary
        what is life without love
        what is death without love

wondering what it all means
with all the worrying
with all the fear
no matter how loud i scream
you won't hear me
cannot hear me

the phone line clicks now
when we speak
you wonder if the phone
is tapped
i say this would be a good thing
since all we speak of is love

moonlight love

he peeled the moon
like an orange
separating it into pieces
she ate each one
slowly
savoring each bite
as if it were the last
once she held the
last slice
in her hand
she passed
it back to him
to consume
so they could
light the sky
together

untitled

he asked if i had a penchant
for red boned brothers with
interesting faces

i don't always see faces
i replied
what do
you
see
he
asked

souls
i said
souls

his request

he wanted to know if i might
consider penciling love
into my day planner

he asked if i would be his wife
if i might want to be loved
if i might need to be held
in between appointments

n.b. envy

she shifted her round head
scrunched her round nose up
and asked, "why you like them
narrow behind men?"

like

behind
closed doors
you
find pleasure
in
my operatic chants
naked dances
and
midnight giggles
that won't stop

smiling
your eyes
read mine
with fascination

how could
a woman
so serious
enjoy life
so much

you wonder

not really
seeking
an answer
to your question

as you turn
out the light

i close
the door

the darkness
brings us
together

killing herself

she had lost the virtue
patience not in the scheme
things seemed to never
occur at the right time
as if divine time were
opposing her very existence
was it a curse
she wondered if it were
some sort of hoo doo
the sins of the father
her father's
evil life massaged into
her hairline along with
the pressing oil big sister used
to make her good hair look
pretty
life more games
than fun
death more inevitable
than ever
she cries
on cue
exactly 3 minutes
before the snooze button

the dance begins
she wishes she were
president so someone
might assassinate her
suicide is for cowards
she thought so instead she
painfully lived on

it's within

he looked for
himself

in store windows
where the clothes
were painted
african/indian/mestizo

he looked for
himself

in the grooves of
a redemption song
dreading his own hair

he looked for
himself

in a langston hughes poem
in a thelonious monk song

that kept getting
louder and louder

he looked for
himself

in the souls of
his sisters

who he caressed
ever so gently
but never touched

he looked for
himself

he cried for the children
the children cried for him

i cried
i cried

the filmmaker

loud music the mask
anxiety painted on his
lips like chap stick

eating too little
sleeping too much
escaping through videos
rented from the corner shop

his couch a cinema complete
with popcorn, cold pizza
people not talking

he never really
believed in love
       it only happens
       in the movies

let me do that

the man from portugal
said he wanted to twist
my hair for me

i sitting with oil and comb
he standing just so with
his hands in my hair
us talking like old friends

he sings a song from
mozambique
i listen
he beatboxes
i rhyme
he places his lips
upon my neck
i move away

i thought you wanted
to twist my hair
            it is you I want
you may twist my hair

i sit again as he stands
just so with comb in hand
he is speaking of mozambique
his music his first loves
he tells me one mustn't be
so practical with matters of
the heart that i discuss relations

as if they were a business matter
i listen

his hands moving from my hair
to my neck as he hums bob marley
he says he enjoys afros and brown skin
while massaging my shoulders
begging me not to leave
i say i must
he says i tease
i say i know

i thought you wanted
to twist my hair
        it is you i want
you said you wanted
to twist my hair.

love sick

    why am i crying
    why   my brain
           knocking at my skull

    why   my voice cracking
    why   my ears ringing

        it hurts

        morning sickness
        at night

        throwing up the pain
        of love

my hands/sore
my heart/burned

i let you in
too soon
now
i ask why

i let you in
too soon
now
it's too late

friends forever

he said we would be friends forever
that he didn't know what he would do
if he could never talk to me again
yet on the outing he wore our
friendship like an old t-shirt
meant for house cleaning, car
washing and general repairs

he said we would be friends forever
that he didn't know what he would do
if he couldn't talk to me again
yet he spoke in a tone as ragged edged
as meat-cutting knives chopping away
at the veins of our connection

he said we would be friends forever
yet he left me standing alone in the
midst of the male chorus that sang
she's too active
she talks too much
she's much too busy

he wiped my tears with
his thumb only to
fertilize the soil in
anticipation of the
storms to come
he brushed his coldness
through my hair
pulling the nappy edges

out from the root
laughing it off
   it's just a joke he said
   just a joke
dancing around my soul
on my heart
in my face as if
we had never just
a year before
he tossed our friendship
into the laundry for the maid
to wash
she unknowingly
hung it out to dry

professor mindsex

there's this
heterosexual intellectual
a mulatto brother
with whom
i've initiated intimacy
he gladly engages
in rough and tumble
incredibly sensual
sessions of mindsex
unexpected moments of
orgasmic dialogue

his left brow rises
like the morning
slowly, i come
to add more honey
my tea needs
sweetening
surrender i tell him
come outside and play
sometimes
living in your head
is a sin

still i'm
a sucker for
his mind
massaging me
in places where
i long to be
touched

booty call

my phone rings with the
sound of male voices
each as lonely as i
hoping for winter warmth
good lovin'
or at least a smile

teasing from time to time
not knowing which to choose
so i choose none
it's too cold to make decisions

he's all right

i hear my man cry
his tears like thumps
on the hardwood floor
he mops them up with
paper towels

hoping no one notices
sobbing into his pillow
secretly wringing it
like a sponge

he loved no one
more than he
loved his mother
he loved her
even more than
he loved himself
he once told me
today he cries

postcard from brooklyn

the bridge is still there
although riding the q train
is quite different
when the train stops on the tracks
my mind flashes back
to the morning i stood with
my stomach in my lap
days later, the smoke still rising
like signals to the gods above
glad you're not here

his royal darkness

skin darker than any i've ever touched
6'7" higher above ground than any i've ever kissed
his presence like summer sun filling up the room
all eyes can't help but be drawn to his majesty

his speech calm. the depth of his voice belies
his youth. he laughs like grandpa, listens like
him too, unafraid to embrace truth.

humility and arrogance collide. this world
is his, but he is ever willing to share. the game of
      love
his to play, but willing to play fair.

this gentle giant displays his artistry over hot
      stoves
and warm pots of tradition from back home—half
      a world
away. a real man, willing to get his hands dirty in
      the kitchen.

his caress, like a daydream. i know what it feels
      like to be held gently by the night.

hi

i've caught him staring
more than once
he's touched my hand twice
and i've slipped attraction
into conversation at least
three times
but who's counting
heartbeats or breaths taken
cannot be measured
when we're in love

lies

lies leap from his lips
lustfully pretending to
reside in truth
they come too easy

a cross between
an angel
and a crow

his big brown eyes
pierce through me
this is too easy for him
for i am transparent

my love for my people
is clear but he cannot
receive it

his house
filled with lies
has no room
for love that
is true

him 3

his silence speaks
loudly of his fears
loving and
being loved

tables turned

i must apologize
for not ending
this bullshit
sooner

i accept total
responsibility
for what has
transpired

i know you
don't believe
it, but
i did
love you

once
maybe
twice

you wondered
why i laughed
so much

it's funny
how simple
you are

unable to
see through
your own
shallowness

never noticing
that i cry
when i laugh

if we look
back i've
been laughing
for the
past four/five/
six months

that's
a lot of
tears
a glance at
my journal
a harsh reminder
of the pain I
endured

i can't explain
what came over me

one morning
i awoke with
this idea

"from now on
i'm gonna love
like a man"

i would fall
asleep holding
my crotch

say i'll call
you knowing
that i wouldn't

i seduced
you on your
coffee table

and excited
homeboy style
mumbling some
bullshit about
spending some
quality time
with the girls

i laughed
all the way
to Traysi's house

we all sat
that evening

listening   Nina Simone
drinking   Heineken
eating   cheesecake
reading   poetry

and laughing
lots of laughing

new Negro?

they used to talk about a new Negro
i want to know what am i

    am i an old negro because
    the new Negro is now old

    OR

    am i a new Negro because i am
    not old enough to be an old negro

    OR

    is it that i was born after the
    new Negro and they called me black

    OR

    is it that i am not black anymore
    since i am African American?

depression

my world
has a sickening sameness
unplanned yet predictable
mother's voice
muffled by the tombstone
above her grave
reeks with reminders
of limitations
hungry fears
suffocating thoughts
causing bodily air
shortages
stiff lungs
and sleepless nights
winning and losing
possess a cynical
oneness
that even the
most creative
imaginations
could not
part separate
or divide

anthem for you

if i could write an anthem for you
and sing it daily
along with my prayers, i would
the whole world standing beside me passionately
harmonizing on your strength and beauty
this anthem, heard from sea to shining sea
ringing through hoods around the world as a daily
    reminder
of the power of the human spirit, truth and love
a heavily funk-infused blues-like number sung in
    the key of life
playing on every radio station promptly at sunrise
a multi-platinum hit promising to be a classic
translated into 13 different languages
everybody sing c'mon
an inspiration to all who have loved and have lost
afraid to love again
this anthem for you
sweeter than coconut bars
dilutes hate in war-torn lands
children in chernobyl drink the juice of your
music and their immune systems are healed
and rejuvenated
all babies have bright futures
and mankind once again believes in dreams
if i could write an anthem
i would sing it daily
along with my prayers
for real, for you
i would

i wonder

the people
were burning
burning alive
burning until
their death
i wonder if
this morning
last night
they had a chance
to say i love
you

every sunday

miss lucy in that
old tired red
velvet hat
struts
the avenue
as if it
were the
nile

true gifts

the gift of his friendship
like none i have loved before

even if it stopped
right here
i could laugh
dance

just
knowing
people like
him exist

for sister sasha

your lips like stone
spoken words tossed like rocks
into the face of gentle human beings
who desire only to be your friend

the weather of life has worn on you
your youthful appearance but a mask
for more pain than anyone would ever imagine

fingers deceivingly angelic
transform into claw-like formations
assassinating characters and ripping
acquaintances into shreds

the men run with good reason
the women who know better
walk out of your path

I see the moon overhead hovering
Like a crow in the distance

Touch your own tenderness
Release the evil and maybe
Then your sun can rise

a picture

flowers
no longer
bloom in the
morning

crisp
rose petals
decorate the
surrounding
area

she
thirsts for
sweet juice
but the roots
are all
dried up

her hands
bleed from
the thorns

a poetic destiny

book fairs book parties
were the norm for this child
sitting as still as any seven-year-old
should or could
and she liked it
peeking in
lurking about
into a world populated by
adults for whom books are
as functional as bathrooms and toothbrushes
studying faces
unknowingly forecasting her future

lady in red sits eyes shut
soaking in the words as if
each were a ray of sunlight
man in blue utters
verbal responses
as if poet and he were
connected in conversation
as if poet were preacher or something
even lines about green trees, brown leaves
and gray eyes
inspired deep from the diaphragm sighs

she watched the way words
worked the room
her first love
language

the woman in white
listening with elegance
long fingers wrapped 'round
her drinking glass
a master of the nonverbals
nodding in perfect harmony
with the melody and rhythm
of every performance

applause
the only thing to shake little miss
wordsmith to be from her daze
the girl learned to count syllables on signs
to pass the time

and she learned to love voices
so she listened
in supermarkets, on street corners at school
she listened

remembering the poet from belgium
he was nigerian
the nigerian from belgium
the sounds of consonants
constantly dancing in her head
the poetry of his presence
at the podium
the resonance of his voice
singing in her mind
she did not need to
understand the meaning of the man's poem
she needed to hear words to watch people
she needed to feel

the timbre of voices in her ears
to breathe
the smell of books
old and new
to taste life
she needed inspiration
which sometimes had little to do with
the poet or even the poem

A Dream Checklist

As I packed to move to New York a couple of years ago, I came across a dream checklist that I had written during my last year of high school. Looking over the list, I was amazed at how many of my dreams I had achieved or was in the process of realizing. Among some of the items on the list: be a poet and have my poems published, record professionally, be on BET, teach, graduate from college, go to London, South Africa, and Paris, live in New York and Senegal, be a great performer, love my own body, and be recognized and respected for the work that I do.

John Muir once said, "The sun shines not on us, but in us." It is through living our dreams, both big and small, that we brighten the earth for all. When I was eight years old I first began writing poetry as a way to soothe my soul. My writing pads became my best friends after my mother's job transferred her from the Bay Area in California to Houston, and helped me cope with the trauma of change.

Fast-forward to college, where I began to partake in poetry again. I mean, poetry as a way of life. It was there that I realized the roots of rap and the potential of it, and everything was connected. Writing raps was a part of writing poetry, a way to tell stories and have my voice heard.

As a scholarship competitor on the speech team, I was required to compete in poetry, prose, and dramatic interpretation, as well as various public speaking events. Those first two years with the speech team were extremely lean ones, during which money was as scarce as peace of mind.

Shawn Raye, a senior member on the team, coached me like a big brother with a firm hand, introducing me to poems as if it were an honor for me to be allowed to know the particular poem he was in love with at the moment. He celebrated tradition and history while boldly questioning them and demanded excellence from anyone who dared recite Pat Parker or June Jordan or Kalamu ya Salaam. We drank poetry like college students downing kegs of beer and took pride in being able to quote Langston's "Dream Deferred" verbatim. Shawn taught me how to make love to and with the word, but his life was unfortunately lost to AIDS and he became the first close friend I lost to the disease. Still, memories of his respect for the poem and pieces of poem were passed on to me before he transitioned, and I hold them near to me as one would a precious family heirloom, something extravagant, meant to be protected and loved.

I decided to make a living at being a poet in November 1992 while I was a student at Howard University. I had just walked away from a good-paying, promising position with a media-training firm and stopped dating someone whose ambitions lay on a path separate from my own. It had all come to a head the day he had taken me to see houses out in the suburbs. There was something about the pale yellow homes, the white picket fences, and the requisite BMW and four-wheel-drive truck in each driveway that had made me feel queasy. And then a friend of his had called for my résumé for a human resources position at a bank and I again was overcome with nausea. I wasn't ready to settle down, to give up on my dreams. I knew I wanted to be an artist—to write, to perform, and to record. So I set out on the next part of my checklist.

I've been able to mark dreams off my checklist because of my willingness to live life day by day, being OK with uncertainty and being willing to create my own thing when it's necessary. I only had one day to decide whether or not to go on my first trip to South Africa. A journalist friend of mine talked about it being one of the most important trips I would make in my life, and he was right, as it opened the door to much of the work that I am doing now. BET called about a *Rap City* interview when I was grieving about a painful betrayal and had literally worried myself sick. I had three days to drink a gallon of water a day, down fresh vegetable juice, steam my nasal passages with eucalyptus, and eat raw garlic. By the time the camera crew arrived, I was still in recovery, but looked great and had enough energy to perform for the duration of the taping. Persistence and hard work enabled me to be prepared for those and other opportunities, which in turn gave me the freedom to work smarter, instead of harder, toward my dreams.

I was so excited that day to find that old dream checklist. It was self-affirming because we often forget to celebrate the little mountains we climb along the way. It was also a reminder for me to keep dreaming, so I took a new sheet of paper, typed "A Dream Checklist" on the top of the page, and did an updated version. I don't look at it every day, but I know that it's there as a guide.

i love short takes . . .

Filling the Cup

One of my mentors says that writers experience life as writers, while others write about life. It's funny because I have ruined many great moments by trying to recount them before they were over and attempting to etch every detail in my mind so that I would retain the beauty of it, hold on to its significance. Today, I caught the bus even though the subway would have been much faster, but the sun was shining and the city seemed to be smiling. I rode it to the end of the line, then walked slowly to the nearest subway, feeling slightly self-indulgent, but remembering something my mentor once said to me about mastering the art of laziness, of doing nothing so the poem might have room to speak. Throughout the years he has shared many words with me, thus no matter how busy I get with performing, traveling, or speaking, I still come back to the page.

Shawn Raye, another one of my big brothers in poetry, first introduced me to E. Ethelbert Miller, whose office in the African American Resource Center on the very top floor of the founders library on Howard University's campus is at once distant and at the center of everything. He sits among the books at his desk ready to fill the cup of hungry, anxious young writers. A brilliant writer in his own right, he is also a critic's critic who has pissed off the best of them, but executes with such class that one must respect his character. Ethelbert is a tough-love type of gentle spirit, honest and as authentic as they come.

I think of him as my literary father because he has been a constant, given unconditionally, and he has spoken his truth whether or not I wanted to hear it. He tells me what he feels I need to hear. Sometimes I listen, sometimes I don't. Once, I dropped off a stack of carefully typed words and returned to find red pen on every page. Ethelbert began to ask questions that I did not have answers to, questions about me, about my words, and about my life. Then he went through each piece, one by one, and by the end of this process I was more than ready to leave his office. He took six pages and circled five lines—about ten words—and told me, "This is the poem."

I studied poetry as an apprentice would, visiting the master craftsman with my most recent piece of handiwork for inspection. He would read, critique, edit, and sometimes even trash the presentation, but I've kept coming back for more over the years. Sometimes he would give me assignments or books that spoke to where I was artistically at the time, so I read Al Young and Haki Madhubuti's work when he was still Don L. Lee. I read Anne Sexton and various poetry anthologies.

But also, as a mentee, I've had to learn to think for myself. A few of my mentors were at one time frustrated with my love for hip hop and my choice to be a "rapper," at one time a bad, bad word in the world of poetry. "You will ruin a potentially great literary career," they said. "You are bigger than that. Better." It angered me greatly at the time and it hurt that these artists from the Black Arts Movement, these once-visionary, revolutionary greats, didn't get it. Now, looking back I see that it was time to cut the umbilical cord and to learn to walk on my own, to think for myself. During this period of distance, I worked hard and stayed committed to my vision, sucking up the pain of what it meant to be a pioneer, committed to the elevation of rap as an artform. The Freestyle Union Artist Development Institute, a structured program for rappers, evolved from this spirit. Hundreds of rappers have benefited from its existence and it became the first full-fledged artist development program focused solely on the art of emceeing. Part of me wonders if I would have worked this hard and stayed committed this long if I had not felt so dissed, like I had something to prove.

Criticism can be hard to swallow even when it's good for you and shared with good intention. Being open to criticism taught me the value of humility, how important it is to listen and to accept others as human beings with their own set of imperfections. Those willing to share with me have shared from a space of love and that can be empowering. My mentor speaks his truth even though it might create conflict or tension. His authenticity taught me to value others who embrace this way of being and gave me something to strive for. Constructive criticism is part of the nourishment needed to evolve into a healthy artist, writer, teacher, and human being.

Mentors have the ability not only to influence our lives, but to shape our destiny. As we journey through life it's important to keep our eyes and ears open for the opportunity to connect with people who might be willing to share their insight and wisdom. Ethelbert has filled my cup for so many years, and in turn, I find myself mentoring other artists, other activists, and those hungry, humble, and willing to listen. Instead of me always dropping by his office, I now have Patty Dukes, a beautiful, massively talented writer/performer, dropping by mine; Derin sending me an e-mail from her Columbia dorm room; or Anthony, Malik, Josh, Wolf, and the rest of my Bronx boys showing up at a workshop. The evolution continues as I attempt to be to them what my mentor has been to me, as each of them allows me to share my gifts, the giving being almost as good as what I have been blessed to receive from my mentor.

let me

let me hold
your hand

let me walk
beside you

let me peek inside
your thoughts

sing you
to sleep

whisper

softly

so you can
barely
hear
my
voice

you
pressing
your
ear
against
my
lips

spell #5

kiss my eyelids

touch my
lashes so
i can
see you

untitled

your smile
like stars
setting the
dark sky
on fire

hope poem #1

build
me
a
world
with

sun
moon
people

willing to vibe

cocoa and you

after midnight
a mug of
cocoa
reminds me of
you

it makes me
hot
all
over

your voice

your voice is making love
on a small bed

curtains blowing
breezes entering
as the jazz
from the radio
sneaks into
our conversation

spell #1

i tried
to write
a poem
about
your eyes

but
you kept
staring
at me

language of love

if i could awake in the middle of the night
and find a poem upon my pillow
i would interrupt each night's sleep
with glee
if i could rise every morning
and find a rhyme upon my doorstep
i would open my home to the world

for jack

your ancestors enslaved mine
but the way you loved me
made me feel incredibly
free

friends

hold
my hand

i'll hold
yours

just walk
slowly

spell #2

your eyes
like
mirrors
i
avoided
looking into
for too long

you

i could count
every star
in the brooklyn sky
and it would still
not add up
to the light
you bring

disguises

sometimes
i cry
sometimes
i scream

laughter
hides
it
all

it's morning

as you played
your horn

i thought
i saw
the sun rise

last night we

laughed
so hard
i must've
hurt my back
and slapped
my brown legs
red

tears
crowded
my brown eyes

different
from the ones
i
shed
this morning

what happened?

inner-course

last
night
i made
love to
myself
for
the
first
time

there was
absolutely
nothing
painful
about
it

luvphobia

roses
cards
calls

he just wanted
her to know
he cared

the early years
living with mother
with father
haunted
her sleep

      mama's eyes red
      daddy's bags packed
      as she left
      for school
      tired
      because she
      spent
      last night
      on her knees
      praying
      the
      fighting
      would cease

recognize

does god
bless us with
exactly what we
need when we need
it or him or what

him

the universe
planted
his presence
precisely
intheright
place,
he came
gently wiping
the sleep
from my
third eye

untitled

the
blessings
love brings
still amaze me

the pouring
of your holy
heart

flooding the
inner sanctums
of my self
and spirit

spell #3

touching your heart
i move closer
wondering
what the rest
of you feels
like

a nighttime short

the night winds howl
when you are not here
but seem to whisper
whenever you are near

fall 6am

the touch
of your hand
in the morning

a smooth
awakening

a little like
peppermint tea

in diamond studded
stoneware mugs

catching
sun's rays
near dawn

looking

each glance
compensates
for your
silence

long stares
stand as
tell tale signs
of mutual adoration

words carry
little weight
with each blink
desire grows

illin'

even though my heart
beats faster before i dial
your number and
my stomach gets knotted
right before i see you
being love sick
never felt so good

no soon come

at first i thought it was me
i couldn't scream
unable to let go
unwilling to be free

i wasn't blocked
putting up walls
or afraid of intimacy

my mind played dumb
but my spirit knew
that who you claimed to be
was not true

Kiss me you fool . . .

And he did
Just like
In the movies
Eyes closed
Souls shaking
Lips lingering

people hurt

the rain burns
my skin
seeping into my
wounds
peace knows not
my name
i scream for help
no one is listening
humanity i love
people i cannot stand

Getting Open

In hip hop there is a term called "getting open"—the next level of creative expression—accessing one's creativity and delivering in a flow that is affecting and inspirational. When one is freestyling (improvising rhymes) one seeks to get open every time one speaks, but it is not always possible to function in the real world and be open every single time.

When one is open the body seems oblivious to the presence of others yet is connected and aware of every movement around one. Some relax into a meditative state while others intensify into a sort of trance, gesturing, rocking back and forth, side to side, or frozen in a stance that allows for the mind, body, and spirit to synthesize. Even more important than the visual of someone getting open are the feelings that are emitted into the air, the excitement, and the impact that energy has on others. I am at my most joyful when that heightened sense of freedom occurs. I get open just thinking about it.

When the mind is heavy at work and thinking just won't stop, getting open is nearly impossible. It is easy to go through the motions and the artist might even fool some of the people some of the time, but deep down she knows something is missing.

I admit it: I get in my own way more often than other circumstances prevent me from getting open. So me, myself, and I now have an agreement to let go, to stay out of the way, and to laugh while we are doing it. Of course, I don't always honor my word, but the key is in how you clean up the mess you have made. For an MC, the hip-hop term used to describe a rapper, a mistake is an opportunity to create a memorable moment, a chance to reveal your humanity and to show just how comfortable you are with yourself and your microphone.

When I facilitate freestyle, improvisational poetry workshops, or impromptu speaking classes, I harp on the point that we must let go of the fear of making fools of ourselves, let go of the fear of looking silly, and not get caught up in what the other people in the room are thinking about us. When we allow ourselves to make mistakes, to say sometimes the "wrong" thing, to not judge ourselves or others, we move closer to our true selves. It is the innocence and willingness of childhood getting blocked by the inflexibility of adulthood, the rigidity of what is right and what is wrong, and the arrogant belief that only one of us knows the "truth" that blocks our genius and inner wisdom. Once we master the skill of letting go and getting open, we can have fun and enjoy the journey.

i love taggin' your heart . . .

The Art of Surrender

Whenever I worried too much one of my ex-
boyfriends would say, "T, let go and let God."
The first time he said this a wave of resentment
crept up my back because I thought he was
questioning my faith. But as I began to practice
surrendering, I began to see the power in
letting go, in silencing my mouth as well as
my mind.

Recently I had a conflict with a friend and
apologized shortly after the incident occurred. He
sent lengthy e-mails to me demanding an apology
not once, but four times. I took a deep breath,
consulted an advisor, and sent a brief, loving,
generous reply stating that I took full responsi-
bility for what had occurred, and although I dis-
agreed with his assessment, I could see how he
felt that way and I apologized for my mistake. He
sent another defensive e-mail, three paragraphs
thick, and this time I wanted to pick up the
phone in response.

His e-mails read like the great voice of God, as
he told me "the truth" about myself, about life,
about what should and what should not be done.
The text lacked compassion, lacked understand-
ing, and reflected so little love that I felt ashamed,
not of him, but of myself. It was a mirror moment
where I saw just how many times I had done the
same thing to someone who I felt had wronged
me. The arrogance of the human spirit can be as

offensive as a bad odor, and damn, did it stink. My immediate impulse was to call him and line by line analyze his writing, to show him his flaws, to highlight the weaknesses in his argument, and to show him just how right I was, but I didn't have the energy. Instead, I surrendered and let go of the need to be right, the need to fight, and the need for him to see my point of view. I had just received a call from a friend whose life-threatening illnesses had her on edge, and that reality check helped me to prioritize what issues in my life needed energy.

He called a week or so later and began the conversation wanting and needing to be right. I put another new skill into practice: answering questions not statements. Surrendering again and again was difficult for me because my instincts are to defend when I perceive an attack, to fight to the death with my tongue as my sword.

Through this process I learned how to let someone be pissed off at me without getting caught up in his or her thoughts. I learned that surrendering is not just for the "big" problems like worrying about your mom's health or your rent payment, but it's also an effective tool for life's daily conflicts.

Sometimes surrendering involves being the "bigger" person, allowing the other to say what is necessary and to experience his or her emotions as they occur, but it's also about knowing when to speak and when to be silent. Time may or may not heal all wounds, but a little time and space can give us room to see a situation from a different perspective.

Oh, and my friend? We are still friends, but we surrendered and are a whole lot tighter now.

the black woman's struggle

her head
swings
low like
sweets'
chariot

but she
ain't comin'
forth to
carry
you home

she and
her sister
carryin'
too much
as it is

the healing power of sickness

she sometimes nursed the tumors
as if they were her young
her stomach swelling with
each moment of stress
the maternity-wear hanging softly
from her thin frame
making her look as if she was expecting
one might say she was
but miracles don't come easily
these days and prayer can
be hard work
she rises early before dawn
hoping that the higher powers
will be less occupied
since most folks are still
sleeping at that time
she talks to herself a lot now
and looks tired
but the forgotten self seems
much happier, more peaceful
in between the fasts, therapy and doctor visits
she treats herself to fruit shakes, good books
and quiet afternoons in busy cafes
alone, well not quite
see, her and her self are learning to
enjoy each other's company
just being and having a good 'ol time

internal inquiry

can i not die from
cancerous causes
can i live to be 99
and die of old age

can i embrace streams
of life blood
where my heart beats
sacred sounds

can i reverse genetic tendencies
toward death and dying
deprogram and recondition habits
unhealthy and
reminiscent of survival

slave food for whose soul

no longer nurturing me
mine yearns for nourishment
as i stand at the place where
selflessness and selfishness
meet

remembering my spirit
feeding my soul
learning to live
languishing on the sandy beaches
of my mind
reaching out to kiss the sun

walking the waters of the earth
with hopes that i may one day
swim toward peace and health
in complete harmony with the universe
facing my creator whole and strong

dust on my shoes

my day ain't right if i don't rise before 10
granddaddy say you greet god
when you greet the sun
so i do

rising early for meditation class
from the shower to the subway to the q train
minutes later frozen on the brooklyn bridge

        people watching
        people screaming
        people watching
        people crying

one wonders if the planes were yawning
if the wings were stretching
if the engine's belly ached
if somebody somewhere instinctively
felt something

i still have dust on my shoes
from standing too close to ground zero
legs still sore from that walk to queens

amidst the manhattan masses
mulling over peace and pain

        is it crazy for me to conceptualize
        a country with courage
        a land that considers violence

might not be the only response
to violence
that one might opt
to give peace
a chance

the pain of this moment too shall pass
the rain hovering, clouds hollering
washing the pain away
shaking us all, waking our souls

rwandan sleep

i fell asleep
on the edge
of my bed
dreaming
about
the face of a
little girl

i swear i've seen
her before
she had big dark
eyes
round & full of an
all too familiar fear

i swear i've seen
her before but
maybe it was
another dream
on another night
when small girls

brown/thin/frightened
didn't spend all
five of their
years on earth
hungry alone
afraid

of being terrorized

our history

the gone years
stand

        nonexistent

young men
women
old mistakes

many
strangers
to our
history

let us hold on
reaping wealth
in knowledge

the past must be
taught relearned
it should not be
relived

the feminine voice in hip hop

i am
an invisible
woman
not
because
people
refuse
to see
me

they know
i am
here
but it's
as if my
woman-ness
detracts
from my existence

my presence
too often
mistaken
for absence

i am
an invisible
woman

whose words
don't flow
fast enough
whose beats
just aren't
phat enough
whose contribution
goes unseen

they know
i am here

because
i was there

i embraced
the music
as he
did

i rocked
the mic
as he
did

i bore
hip hop
as he
did

we/nurtured
it

i am
an invisible
woman

i may not
be seen

i'll be
damned
if i
won't
be heard

i wOman

this year
will always
be memorable

       i became
       a woman

only this
time it ain't
got nothin'
to do with
candlelight
and luther

ain't got
nothin'
to do
with teasing
touching

sunday dinners

the foyer possessed that old
southern baptist church aroma
while
mother gray's breath spoke
of black velvet or some other
whiskey-like beverage
the old women bathed
in the latest line of
avon perfumes
walking regally down the aisle
most migrating from
louisiana, mississippi and texas
which explains the hog head cheese
gumbo and lingering hints of perfectly
fried chicken in the banquet hall
their wide hips tell stories of hot water
cornbread sizzling in cast iron skillets
crackling to the rhythm of
grandma's heart songs
who so proudly cooks
up enough for everyone
i slip some sundays
turning on the radio
leaving it on the gospel station
being drawn in by the
depth of old church hymns
spirituals and baptism songs

my heart follows a path back
to childhood days

the old folks moaning so much
you'd swear no one knew the words
                    precious lord
music transporting me for only a moment
filling me with calm and warmth
and although hog head cheese doesn't
fit into my vegetarian lifestyle and the
traditional church
doesn't seem to provide me
with spiritual food
i cherish the memories
of california country
old women in big velvet hats
amens and hallelujahs
and little fingers covered with
chicken grease and cornbread

show me (the talk is cheap blues)

don't write
me no
oh
beautiful
black woman
how lovely
you are poem

don't write
me a
nubian princess
queen of the nile song

don't write me
no poem 'bout
the appeal of my dark skin
or a song about the bliss
you are in

don't even
talk to
me or
utter a word

i don't see myself
in their magazines
or your videos

my likeness
I find in

my mirror

i have read
your poems

i have heard
your words

it is the doing
that i long for

the act
of being
       feeling
       appreciated
       admired

i've worked
hard to
become who
i am

i know
my beauty
but your
actions
sometimes
make me
ask

do you

accident at the church

the steeple
toppled into the
parking lot

causing the
parishioners
to scream

to actually
care about
one another

this time of year

the almost red
orange leaves
captivate
the little girl
in me

October days
were the best
days

cool morning frost
not so warm sun
socks/long sleeves
oatmeal cookies
in the oven

family tales

grandpa
usedta say

when you visit a
stranger's home make

sure you don't sit on
their toilets

don't lay your head
on their pillows

and by all means
don't drink the water

unless it's in
a glass

even then
you might not

see what's going
on

slowdancewithdeath/life

lips cracked
dry from winter air
my skin gray
walking dead
among the commuters
hoping no one can see me
i want to be invisible today
unseen by the many who
look and wonder
what became of her
in my absence i am
here but no one notices
the lonely until it is too late
my hair uncombed
covered by silk scarf
and a hat
insurance so no one
sees me
my clothes oversized
my shoes worn
i rationalize that there
is power in being invisible
underestimated and unnoticed
hiding my beauty and myself
i tell my therapist i am angry
crying about my mother who is dead
my big sister who is also angry
clinging to sickness i am comfortable
at home with remedies and recipes
to make me well yet at the core i resist

it, this wellness thing, if i am healed
i will be forced to live in this sick world
and what kind of life would that be
if i move slowly no one will notice
it was suicide

power of emotion

every so often when lying down at night
i get this sudden urge
to pray
get out of bed
get down on my knees
and pray

every so often when sitting on my bed
unable to control it i start
to cry
sometimes i know why i'm crying
sometimes i don't
so i just cry

every so often when looking out of the window
i can see the whole world
i take it into my arms
trying
to hug the hurt away

got it bad

i find myself blushing ·
at my own thoughts
he's so easy on the eyes

pondering his sexiness
has me singing
blues songs of

i got it bad
i got it bad

praise poem for what we shared

did we not cling to one another
as if the wind would cease to blow
as if rain would choose not to visit
while the sun would only peek through
the clouds

we did not could not let go
our hearts tugged like a thugged
out romance of street love
tic for tac one step forward
two steps back

like kids running away into the night
only to find themselves at grandma's
ten blocks away from home

ours was a necessary kind of love
like teething, potty training
or the awkwardness of adolescence
we needed our oneness

as wrong as it was at times
it was right
for us

the pain
(toni blackman intro for kelly bell album)

my life—a never-ending blues song
bears an uncanny resemblance to the face of god
my mama's pain-filled screams
echo in the halls of eternity
for my birth was not my beginning
but the blackhuman
continuum kicking fiercely
fighting ferociously fearlessly
belting out the blues
phat and as long as
forever
the waters may be muddy
the wolf may howl but the pain
is king b.b. b.boy
and phat
blusicians of the world unite
do right—let the pain lead you to the
light nin' hopkins
would say it's a sin
to diss one's own kin
phat blues bringing
your friendly neighborhood grooves
to your doorstep and your heart
blues as brown as ruth
gimme that ol' time religion
for i am a witness
see, big mama thornton's hound dogs
bark during my pain-filled prayers

so don't ask me why i like my blues phat
ring my bell kelly
so i can feel the pain
place my blues upon the pulpit
preach poetic profundities
pass on particularly powerful prophecies
to the next generation
let us bow our heads
in tribute to this
cosmic commune

prayer:
oh great one greater and bluer than you and i.
i solemnly swear, promise and pledge to perpetu-
ally put forth the pain, to bring the pain as sure as
the sky . . . so phat . . . so blue . . . as it too plays my
song . . . phat blues shall blare through the soular
system rising and setting like the sun, bearing
fruit like the trees, giving birth to life and loud
pain-filled screams resounding clearly in the heav-
ens above. transbluescent and clear. phat blues is
here. ring my bell kelly. just so i can feel the pain.

for those who chant the pussy song

obsessed with
vaginal chants of
regions of
acts of nonsense

not moving us forward
stagnant we remain
clutching
to those concepts
with which they have
brainwashed us
with which they have
controlled us

sex
can be/hypnotic if
you allow it to be

sex
can be/an escape if
you allow it to be

the only true
escape from reality is
death

and
we are allowing
it
to happen
one by one by one

we
are endangered
species

sex
is not for
us people
we cannot allow
it
to happen

we
must
make love

tagging your heart not walls

for kalamu ya salaam

hip hop is not music
it is not dance
it is not djing or writing
it is not rhyming
no voice is needed
hip hop is not beats
it is not the
    boom bap, the boom-boom bap
but the way the
    boom bap
feels when it vibrates through
ooh
hip hop is not song
nor is it singing
or even speaking
it is not windmills
it is not 12-inch vinyls
or 16-ounce cans of krylon paint
it is tagging
your heart
not walls
it is feeling
it is not hard core
or soft
it is not old school
or new
it is not east, west
or even worldwide
it is within

twenty

childhood
     a faint thought
high school
     a concrete memory
distant pictures of the past
     flashingflickering
visions of the girl
     seeking
          searching
               struggling
discovering
     the woman

i wish part 1

i wish i could separate
my thoughts
place each one in its
own compartment
shatter white noise
caused by mental chaos
then release them like
abandoned dreams

in my mind's eye
i dance naked without
inhibition
my flesh ripe like fruit
sweet to the touch
cools the hand
heals the heart

somewhere in some
distant land
suppressed voices
also rummage through
the sky looking for
stars, hope
sanity

in this life

the war rages on
man versus man
versus machine
it seems to be a
never ending
battle

the struggle for power
control of what belongs to
none of us

how does one begin
a peaceful journey
in a world filled
with so much anger
hate makes it hard to
understand the next man

everyone wanting to be right
makes doing wrong a guilt-free activity

as peace eludes us in this lifetime
one can't help but wonder if
there is enough time to save
us from ourselves
or is self destruction
inevitable

life lessons

the burden of the bright
the strong, the beautiful
must be a joke up in heaven
angels gathering around the tube
for primetime

gifts come with price tags

brilliance can cause a glare
even in the eyes of the one shining

i quit

loving
you felt
like a job

with
no perks
no benefits
no vacation

please
accept
this
letter
of resignation

do i have to? (verse 1)

i woke up early in the morning with the pain on
    my mind
the thoughts see i just couldn't leave them
    behind
my stomach didn't feel quite right
i tossed and turned all night
tried to sleep tight
but i rose with the sunlight
my heart cried, but i couldn't find the tears
so scared i seemed to be running from my own
    fears
years and years of ish on my shoulders
i'm closer to success, but the world seems colder
looking for my center, but all i find are splinters
in my skull, these bootstraps i can't seem to pull
on my own, damn, i thought 28 meant you were
    grown
but humbling experiences are all that i am shown
i take a nose dive deep into my soul
but i'm only treading water when swimming is
    the goal
i sit upon the rock, but i can't find the roll
i was going east looking for the north pole
mass confusion, chaotic intrusions, keep bruising
my heart; is there a book on how to heal it
get back to the start
you know the day, your first birthday
innocent pure before being poisoned by the
    world's way

the pleasantries they get displayed, but when we
     do that
from the truth we have strayed
so you ask how i'm doing and i say fine
in one day i done lied for the ninth time

chorus:
i think about all the pain i feel inside
i think about all the tears i done cried
playing in this game to win i've tried
my heart still beats, but many times i've died

Love: I Hate Valentine's Day

I told a fellow artist that the title of my book was initially going to be *I Hate Valentine's Day*, after one of my poems, and his response was "You've got issues." I laughed and asked, "Don't we all?" The words first came to me when I was living in an all-female dorm while attending Howard University. Working as a resident assistant provided me with free housing, but I had to do duty at the front desk, where every male guest had to sign in with me. So there I sat one Valentine's Day manning the desk, watching several young women transform into saddened, lonely beings. One cried because the flowers never came while another cursed because the flowers were not roses. One girl told a guy off because the teddy bear was from 7-Eleven while another sat at my post with me the whole time because she could not stand to be alone on Valentine's Day. Some friends quietly joked (and complained) about not having a valentine and others went out with men whom they did not even like just so they could say they had a date. In exploring how one day could have such a negative impact on so many people, one need only turn to the commercials and advertisements, the merchandise and all the seeds that are planted in our wounded souls.

The idea of "I Hate Valentine's Day" is not about hating anything, but about loving ourselves enough to strip away the warped ideas we have about love. There are so many stereotypes, generalizations, and misconceptions about what love is, and even though I cannot necessarily say that I know what love is, I can say that I know what love feels like. It's not just a spine-tingling, heart-pounding high, but also the warmth that comforts like a cup of orange-cinnamon tea. True love makes it easy to stand with your feet firmly planted on the ground because within that space, you can roam about freely through life, free to fall if necessary, knowing that it's okay.

Sometimes I wonder if we can truly define and simplify an emotion so encompassing and magnanimous. I mean, really define love. Who would give either you or me the power to do such a thing? We could attempt to explain it, but our choice of words would probably change tomorrow. The way in which we chose to define it would have to be based upon our own experiences and where we are on our journey in this moment, right now, today. Love might be one thing today and another the next.

I feel a certain pang of guilt about trying to define love, but it is a topic that needs to be explored more often. Be honest now, when someone says "love," most of us jump automatically to thoughts of romantic love, in the sense of girl-friend, boyfriend, husband, or wife, but over the past few years I have begun to digest and process feelings differently, from a different space. I am touched by memories of my students at the Barry Farms writing project, where I taught with WritersCorps while living in Washington, D.C., years ago, and today by what I see in the eyes of

the kids at Robert F. Wagner High School in
Queens. I tell them I love them often because I
do. I feel the love my fourteen-year-old nephew
has for me when he walks into the room. I have
friends who love me unconditionally, with all of
my flaws and imperfections, and mentors who I
know are surrogate parents for life. I also have ex-
boyfriends who tell me they love me and a cur-
rent flame I love so much it wouldn't matter if we
were "together" as a couple or not. The love and
the friendship are impenetrable and deeper than
anything else.

My last ray of hope for real love directs me
away from the specific issues and toward the more
general concern of love or the lack thereof. Com-
ing of age has provided me with a front row seat
to reality and what it means to have relationships.
Both platonic and romantic relationships are
plagued with dishonesty, betrayal, jealousy, inse-
curity, and other aspects of human nature. Good-
ness and honesty are special and rare instead of
regular and normal. Understanding and nonjudg-
ment are far from being common characteristics
in our exchanges with other people. If love and
fear are the two basic emotions, then more love or
a better understanding of it would provide us with
at least an inch of growth toward making this
world a better and more peaceful place to exist.

I admit that my piece "I Hate Valentine's Day"
is probably not my favorite, but I know that it
speaks to people, lots of them. My good friend
and music producer in Paris, Shay Mane, created
house and garage tracks for the text that spin on

radio overseas. I've performed it with several different bands, to several kinds of music, at the Lilith Fair and when I opened for Rickie Lee Jones. We even used it in a hip-hop theater performance at Dance Place in Washington, D.C., a few years ago. The words were written to provoke thought, to inspire action, and to serve as a reminder of self-love. I think I hear it differently each time I perform it, as an affirmation of sorts. In the world of music, there's a song that says, "Last night a DJ saved my life," but in my world I think it was the DJ—and a poem. I Hate Valentine's Day.

In 2001, TONI BLACKMAN was named Hip-Hop
Ambassador by the U.S. State Department, and as
such has served as artist-in-residence in Senegal,
Ghana, and South Africa. She has performed in
Angola, England, France, and all over the United
States. Blackman has opened for the likes of Mos
Def, the Roots, Wu-Tang Clan, Passi, and Rickie
Lee Jones. A Lilith Fair Talent Search winner and
winner of the Capitol Records Girls Room Tour,
Blackman is also the moderator for Kevin Pow-
ell's Hip Hop Speaks lecture series. Founder of
the Freestyle Union, a Motown-like training
ground for rappers with an emphasis on social
responsibility, she has worked with legendary
guitarists Vernon Reid and James "Blood" Ulmer
and French opera singer Aria, and is currently
working with pianist Danilo Perez. This musical
ambassador for A Round World Productions loves
to push the envelope through collaborations with
artists from Senegal, Haiti, Ireland, Tibet, the
Congo, and China. Early in 2003 she attended
the SeneRAP International Hip-Hop Festival
where she rocked with the world's best in hip
hop, and she is scheduled to record in France,
Burkina Faso, and New York. *Inner-course* is her

first book. For news, book events, and updates on Toni Blackman and to contact her, visit her website, www.toniblackman.com.